THE STORY OF THE
NEW ORLEANS

CREATIVE EDUCATION

Published by Creative Education
123 South Broad Street
Mankato, Minnesota 56001
Creative Education is an imprint of The Creative Company.

DESIGN AND PRODUCTION BY **EVANSDAY DESIGN**

PHOTOGRAPHS BY Getty Images (Allsport, Andrew D. Bernstein / NBAE, Chris Birck / NBAE, Cosmo Condina, Jonathan Daniel / ALLSPORT, Tim Defrisco, Garrett W. Ellwood / NBAE, Barry Gossage / NBAE, Andy Hayt / NBAE, Joe Murphy / NBAE, NBAE, Gregory Shamus, David Sherman / NBAE), SportsChrome (L. Johnson, Michael Zito)

LIBRARY OF CONGRESS CATALOGING-IN-PUBLICATION DATA

Gilbert, Sara.
The story of the New Orleans Hornets / by Sara Gilbert.
p. cm. — (The NBA: a history of hoops)
Includes index.
ISBN-13: 978-1-58341-417-0
1. New Orleans Hornets (Basketball team)—History—
Juvenile literature. I. Title. II. Series.

GV885.52.N375G55 2006
796.323'64'0976335—dc22   2005051201

First edition

9 8 7 6 5 4 3 2 1

COVER PHOTO: *Chris Paul*

THE STORY OF THE
NEW ORLEANS
HORNETS

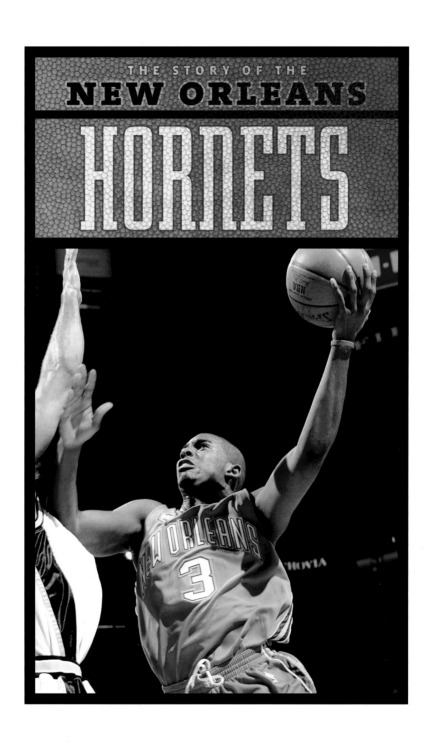

SARA GILBERT

CREATIVE C EDUCATION

The Hornets' Alonzo Mourning

WASN'T AFRAID OF ANYBODY. THE 6-FOOT-10 AND 260-POUND CENTER FEARLESSLY MUSCLED HIS WAY TO THE HOOP AGAINST LARGER, MORE EXPERIENCED PLAYERS, LEADING THE HORNETS TO A PLAYOFF BERTH IN 1993. EVEN WHEN THEY DREW THE FAVORED BOSTON CELTICS IN THE FIRST ROUND, "'ZO" REFUSED TO BACK DOWN. "BOSTON'S GOT ALL THOSE CHAMPIONSHIPS," MOURNING SAID. "BUT THEY DIDN'T WIN ANY OF THEM AGAINST US." WITH FOUR-TENTHS OF A SECOND LEFT IN GAME 4, MOURNING SANK A 20-FOOT JUMPER TO WIN THE SERIES FOR THE UNDERDOGS AND ETCH A GOLDEN MOMENT IN HORNETS HISTORY.

THE FIRST YEARS

1

SINCE ITS BEGINNINGS, NEW ORLEANS HAS BEEN A city with many identities. Although originally named in honor of French regent Duc d'Orleans, it has also been known as the Crescent City, The City that Care Forgot, and The Big Easy. No matter what it's called, New Orleans is certainly a city that knows how to have fun. It's the birthplace of jazz and the home of the annual Mardi Gras celebration.

Adding to this energy is the town's love of professional sports, especially basketball. In the 1970s, the city was briefly the home of a National Basketball Association (NBA) team called the Jazz, which moved to Utah in 1979. Twenty-three years later, pro basketball returned in the form of a team called the Hornets.

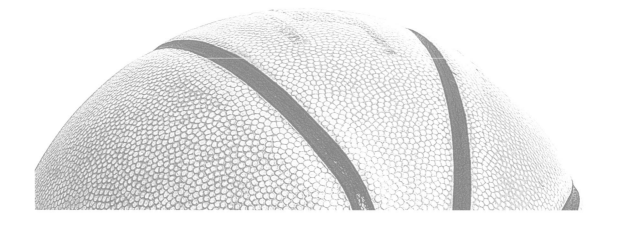

HORNETS

Tiny but talented point guard Muggsy Bogues was a big part of the early history of the Charlotte Hornets

J.R. Reid played college ball at the nearby University of North Carolina before joining Charlotte in 1989

The Hornets franchise started out in Charlotte, North Carolina, in 1988. Although most of the original Hornets were either old or inexperienced, fans appreciated the play of veteran guard Tyrone "Muggsy" Bogues, a 5-foot-3 and 140-pound offensive sparkplug, and Rex Chapman, a guard whom the Hornets selected with their first-ever draft pick. "Rex can shoot, he can drive, and he can jump out of the gym," noted Charlotte coach Dick Harter. Unfortunately, the team had few other weapons and finished just 20–62 that first season.

Despite the addition of forward J.R. Reid, the Hornets got off to a miserable 8–32 start in 1989–90. Harter was replaced by assistant Gene Littles, who tried to jumpstart the team with a fast-break offense. The young Hornets struggled to adjust to the up-tempo style and went 26–56 in 1990–91. Unable to boost Charlotte out of the Eastern Conference cellar, Littles resigned after the season. The Hornets needed some heroes.

BUSY AS BEES The 1987 decision to name Charlotte's basketball team the Hornets actually had little to do with stinging insects. Rather, the name came from the annals of history. During the American Revolutionary War, after British general Charles Cornwallis captured Charlotte, the city's citizens wreaked so much havoc upon the English army by firing at soldiers as they went out for supplies that General Cornwallis was reported to have said, "There's a rebel behind every bush. It's a veritable nest of hornets." More than 200 years later, the city bestowed the name on its new NBA franchise. The Hornets name has long been popular in Charlotte; it was also used at one time by the city's minor league baseball club and its World Football League team.

A STRONGER STING

UNDER NEW COACH ALLAN BRISTOW, THE HORNETS'
luck began to change. In 1991, they drafted 6-foot-7
forward Larry Johnson, who promptly averaged 19
points and 11 rebounds per game and earned the NBA
Rookie of the Year award. And in 1992, Charlotte drafted
Alonzo Mourning, a 6-foot-10 and 260-pound center with
strength, agility, and an intense attitude. "Most rookies
are a little intimidated coming into this league," said
Bristow. "'Zo never backs down from anybody."

With Johnson and Mourning anchoring the front line,
and Bogues and sweet-shooting swingman Dell Curry
handling the ball, the Hornets surged into the playoffs
in 1993. The young Hornets were underdogs in their
matchup against the Boston Celtics, but they were brim-
ming with confidence. The Celtics won the first game
of the series, but Charlotte took the next three, with
Mourning hitting the series-clinching shot in Game 4.
Although Charlotte was eliminated by the New York
Knicks in the second round, the Hornets seemed to be
on their way.

13

HORNETS

A quick and explosive scorer, forward Larry Johnson looked more like a boxer than a basketball player

BASKETBALL

Alonzo Mourning had a knack for clearing space under the rim as he battled for points and rebounds

Thrilled by his young team's rise to prominence, Hornets owner George Shinn rewarded Johnson with a 12-year, $84-million contract extension in 1993—the most lucrative deal in league history. But early in the 1993–94 season, Johnson suffered a back injury and missed almost half of the season. Mourning was sidelined with injuries for several weeks as well. The Hornets rallied around Bogues and Curry to post a respectable 41–41 record, but they came up short of the playoffs.

Mourning blossomed into a superstar upon his return the next season, averaging 21 points and nearly 10 rebounds per game. The Hornets won 50 games for the first time in franchise history but were eliminated in the playoffs by the Chicago Bulls. After the season, Mourning asked to be paid like the All-Star he had become. Unable to afford another costly contract, the Hornets traded him and two other players to the Miami Heat, getting high-scoring forward Glen Rice, point guard Khalid Reeves, and center Matt Geiger in return.

GRANDMAMA JOHNSON

With his wide shoulders and bulging biceps, Larry Johnson was an imposing figure on the basketball court. But it didn't bother the burly Hornets forward to put on a floral-print dress, horn-rimmed glasses, a strand of pearls, and a pillbox hat over a fluffy gray wig. Dressed as "Grandmama" for a comical series of commercials for Converse basketball shoes, Johnson put opponents to shame. "These are my new shoes from Converse," he said in one ad. "They're so light and fast, even my Grandmama can whoop you in them." Then Johnson, dressed as his own Grandmama, complete with a gold tooth, dunked on quivering opponents, saying, "Remember—you can't beat what you can't catch." The television spots aired in 1994, but they still rank as one of the most successful sports advertising campaigns.

CHANGES AT THE TOP

THE HORNETS STRUGGLED AFTER THE TRADE. AFTER they missed the playoffs in 1996, Coach Bristow was fired and replaced by Dave Cowens, and Johnson was traded to the New York Knicks for muscular forward Anthony Mason. Charlotte continued to reshuffle its lineup by acquiring 7-foot-1 center Vlade Divac in a trade with the Los Angeles Lakers.

Many fans expected the new-look Hornets to struggle. But the team bucked the odds, thanks in large part to Rice, who averaged almost 27 points a game and proved himself one of the league's deadliest three-point shooters. Charlotte finished with a franchise-best 54–28 record, but the cheers quickly died as the Knicks swept the Hornets in the first round of the playoffs.

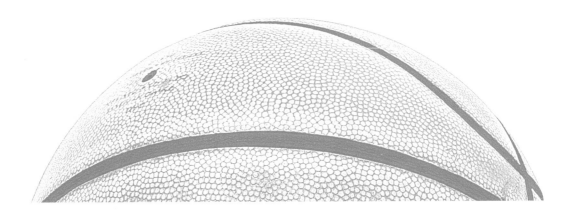

HORNETS

Anthony Mason used his great strength to pull down 22 rebounds in one game during the 1996–97 season

18

Before becoming Charlotte's coach, Paul Silas was one of the NBA's best defensive players of the 1970s

The next season, Charlotte traded Bogues to the Golden State Warriors and signed guards David Wesley and Bobby Phills. This new backcourt led the Hornets to a 51–31 record and a first-round playoff win over the Atlanta Hawks before the Chicago Bulls brought Charlotte's season to an end. "We played hard, but we've still got a ways to go to be a champion," said Cowens.

When the Hornets started just 4–11 in 1998–99, Cowens was replaced as head coach by assistant Paul Silas. Silas had earned a reputation as a fierce competitor during his NBA playing days, and he quickly conveyed his never-say-die attitude to the team. "Paul told us we could sit around and lick our wounds, or we could go out and make something of our season," explained Wesley. The team responded. After making a trade for swingman Eddie Jones and center Elden Campbell, Charlotte won 22 of its last 35 games and just missed the playoffs.

With the addition of explosive rookie point guard Baron Davis, the Hornets had high hopes for the 1999–00 season. Sadly, early in the season, a car accident claimed the life of veteran guard Bobby Phills. The Hornets honored their fallen friend by fighting to a strong 49–33 finish. But in the playoffs, Charlotte fell to the Philadelphia 76ers.

THE LITTLE GUY

At 5-foot-3, Tyrone "Muggsy" Bogues was the shortest player in NBA history. But he never let his lack of height hold him back. During his 10 seasons with the Charlotte Hornets, he became one of the most popular players on the team, despite the fact that he never averaged more than 11.1 points per game. His jersey was as popular with kids as those of All-Star teammates Alonzo Mourning and Larry Johnson, and in 1997 he was ranked the ninth-most popular NBA player in *Sports Illustrated for Kids*—just behind stars such as Scottie Pippen and Magic Johnson. But it wasn't just kids who appreciated Bogues. Teammates adored him, opponents respected him, and coaches counted on him. "He's the heartbeat of our team," Hornets head coach Allan Bristow once said.

21

HORNETS

David Wesley wore a Hornets uniform for eight seasons, averaging at least 13 points a game every year

MASHBURN IN THE MIX

THE HORNETS SPENT THE NEXT YEAR TRYING TO assemble a winning mix of new talent. In the 2000 NBA Draft, they chose rugged forward Jamaal Magloire from the University of Kentucky. After that, they put together trades that brought forwards P.J. Brown and Jamal Mashburn to town as well.

A rock-solid rebounder, forward P.J. Brown was an unsung hero with his aggressive inside play

LOADERS

Jamal Mashburn exploded for 50 points in one game during the 2002-03 season, setting a team record

Fans hoped that these players would make the 2001–02 season one to remember. It was a season to remember, but for the wrong reasons. Mashburn, the player counted on more than any other to lead the team, missed most of the season due to injury. Worse, it was made public that the Hornets were likely playing their last season in Charlotte. The team's owners claimed that the Hornets were not making enough money in Charlotte to remain competitive and had decided to move the club to New Orleans.

Since the NBA would not grant final approval of the move until May 2002, Charlotte players, coaches, and fans faced an uncertain future. Still, the team was not ready to pack it in. Mashburn returned to the lineup late in the season and exploded for 21 points a game to power the Hornets back to the playoffs. Davis then stepped up to lead the team to a three-games-to-one series win against the Orlando Magic, posting triple-doubles (double-digit statistics in points, rebounds, and assists) in Games 3 and 4. But the New Jersey Nets eliminated Charlotte in the second round, and the Hornets headed to New Orleans.

LOSING BOBBY PHILLS

On January 12, 2000, Hornets guard Bobby Phills got into his car after a team practice at the Charlotte Coliseum and drove away. But he didn't get far. Less than a mile from the arena, he collided head-on with an oncoming vehicle and was killed instantly. Phills's death shocked the team, especially after witnesses reported seeing him racing his Porsche against teammate David Wesley at high speeds. After a police investigation, Wesley was charged with reckless driving and speed competition. He joined his teammates in wearing black patches on their jerseys but avoided talking about Phills's death for almost a year. "There hasn't been a day that I haven't thought about him and relived that accident," Wesley said in 2001. "He is always in my heart."

A NEW HIVE

EXPECTATIONS WERE HIGH FOR THE HORNETS' inaugural season in the Big Easy, and the team did not disappoint. On opening night, the Hornets took on New Orleans' former team, the Utah Jazz. Davis scored 21 points, and Mashburn grabbed 10 rebounds in a 100–75 victory. The celebration continued as the team then won 10 more straight games at home. Magloire established himself as a tough rebounder and fierce shot blocker, and Mashburn stayed healthy enough to play in all 82 games for the first time in his NBA career. The Hornets finished their first New Orleans season 47–35 before losing to the Philadelphia 76ers in the first round of the playoffs.

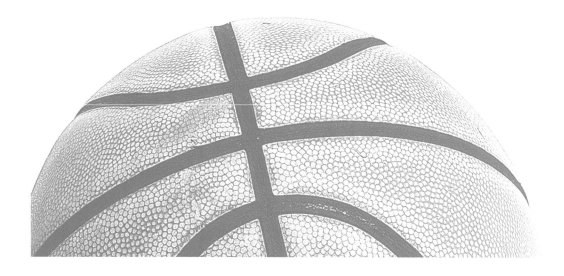

27

HORNETS

Jamaal Magloire handled much of the Hornets' dirty work, including fighting for rebounds and setting picks

NBA

A bulldog of a point guard, Baron Davis directed New Orleans' offense with great energy and confidence

Davis and Magloire were the leading stories of season number two in New Orleans, as each put up All-Star efforts to carry the team back to the playoffs. But the Hornets were knocked out in the first round again, this time by the Miami Heat. "We couldn't get into any kind of rhythm," said Hornets guard David Wesley after New Orleans lost Game 7. "We couldn't make any runs."

The hard-fought battle against the Heat seemed to take the wind out of the Hornets' sails. The team started the 2004–05 season with former NBA star Byron Scott as its new head coach, but fans were left stunned by a trade that sent Baron Davis—the team's best player—to the Golden State Warriors for guard Speedy Claxton. Without Davis, the Hornets stumbled to an 18–64 record, the worst in franchise history.

The silver lining to that bad record was that it helped the Hornets secure the fourth overall pick in the 2005 NBA Draft. With it, they selected Chris Paul, an All-American from Wake Forest University whom many basketball experts expected to become the NBA's next star point guard. "He has great leadership skills," New Orleans general manager Allan Bristow said. "We feel he can be a part of an explosive young backcourt for us."

Since joining the NBA almost two decades ago, the Hornets have experienced highs, lows, tragedies, and a relocation. Yet through all of the ups and downs, they have always fought with a determination befitting their name. Now, as they build a new hive of fans and excitement in New Orleans, the Hornets plan to soon swarm over an NBA title.

Chris Paul lived up to the hype in 2005–06, leading all NBA rookies in both points and assists per game

DESIGNER DUDS

When it came time to dress the Charlotte Hornets, team owner George Shinn had one man in mind: Alexander Julian, an award-winning menswear designer and North Carolina native. To create the team's uniforms, Julian paired bright teal with purple, added pinstripes, and put pleats on the shorts. The design was enormously popular with fans and was one of the top NBA apparel sellers for years. But Julian, who has since designed uniforms for the University of North Carolina basketball teams, wasn't in it for the money. The only payment he wanted was a "down-home barbecue," which he said was impossible to find in New York City. The Hornets agreed to send him five pounds of pork barbecue from Papa Doc's Pig Palace every month—and when they were late, Julian sent an overdue notice.

INDEX